IT'S YOUR STORY—TELL IT!
AN AMBASSADOR
LEADERSHIP JOURNEY

bliss
live it !

the dove
self-esteem
fund

Photographs/Quotes/Lyrics

Side A: Page 6: quote from *The Wisdom of Eleanor Roosevelt* by Donald Wigal. © 2003 Philosophical Library, Inc. All rights reserved. Reprinted by arrangement with Kensington Publishing Corp.; **Pages 9, 31, 41, 44, 56, 60:** cyanotypes and photographs by Ann Giordano © 2002-2010. All rights reserved; **Page 14:** John Lund/Getty Images; **Page 30:** "Dream Operator" written by David Byrne. Courtesy of Index Music, Inc.; **Page 50:** Varial Studio; **Page 51:** Sonali Srridhar and Solargold is a collaboration with Emilie Grenier; **Page 55:** Catherine Haight

Side B: Page 16: Todd Korol/Getty Images; **Page 30:** Lawrence Lawry/Getty Images

This publication was made possible by a generous grant from the Dove Self-Esteem Fund.

WRITTEN BY Wendy Russell Thomas, Laura J. Tuchman, Andrea Bastiani Archibald, Valerie Takahama, and Deborah Reber

ILLUSTRATED BY Anika Starmer, Michael Wertz

DESIGNED BY Pamela Geismar, Elizabeth Van Itallie, and Lisa Beres for Charette Communication Design.

EXECUTIVE EDITOR: Laura J. Tuchman

ART & PRODUCTION: Douglas Bantz, Ellen Kelliher, Sarah Micklem, Sheryl O'Connell, Lesley Williams

DIRECTOR, PROGRAM RESOURCES: Suzanne Harper

Text printed on Fedrigoni Cento 40 percent de-inked, post-consumer fibers and 60 percent secondary recycled fibers.

Covers printed on Prisma artboard FSC Certified mixed sources.

Mixed Sources
Product group from well-managed forests and other controlled sources
www.fsc.org Cert no. SQS-COC-100209
© 1996 Forest Stewardship Council
FSC

WANTED: DREAM-SEEKERS

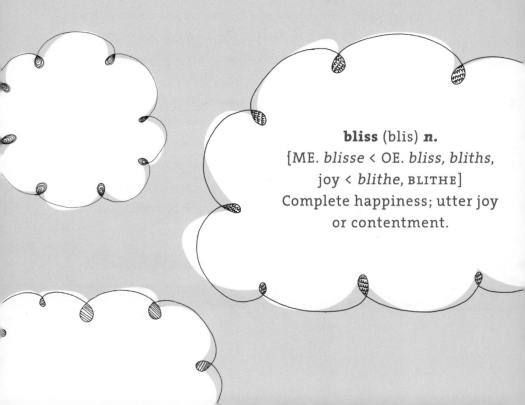

bliss (blis) **n.**
[ME. *blisse* < OE. *bliss, bliths,*
joy < *blithe,* BLITHE]
Complete happiness; utter joy
or contentment.

WANTED:
DREAM-SEEKERS

By now, you're probably a seasoned dreamer. Maybe you've dreamed of winning a major election, or standing on an Olympic podium, or wiping out the flu virus once and for all.

Maybe you've pictured yourself working for a cause you care about deeply.

Maybe you've fantasized about being free of all things that trouble you, or earning your way to spending your days exactly as you please—writing the novel you know is inside you, painting the landscapes you've carried with you since your first trip to the mountains. Ah, bliss!

As you near your move from high school to the next phase of your life, the decisions you make will become part of the course you plot for yourself as a woman and a leader—in your daily life and in the world around you. This journey sees to it that your dreams—those you're willing to work for—play a starring role in that future. It encourages you to dream big, as all leaders do, and it gives you the tools to do so.

All along *bliss*, you will:

* **dig into your personal standards and values to see how they make you you, and how they can form the foundation of your dreams.**

* **explore your strengths and passions. How can these important parts of yourself be translated into your dreams?**

* **dip into stories of dreams and dreamers all around you—and tell your own dream stories, too! After all, sharing these stories is one of the best ways for them to come true.**

Life is full of twists and turns. Some may frustrate or confuse you. Others can open doors to wonderful, new adventures—and wonderful, new dreams! Navigating them all builds your confidence to push through whatever life throws at you. And by doing so, you'll better understand yourself—your needs and desires, and, ultimately, how to realize your dreams! So throughout this journey to *bliss*, embrace change! It may be the key to your dreams and your bliss, and the full story of you!

**The future belongs
to those who believe in the
beauty of their dreams.**

—ELEANOR ROOSEVELT

YOUR TICKET TO DREAMLAND

Dreams could be described as the faraway thoughts of a free mind. During sleep, dreams are the jumble of stories that race through your subconscious. But when you're awake, you dream, too—about what you want from life. You may already have a full story in your mind of what you want your ideal future to be.

You may have short-term dreams (to win the part of Ophelia in a school production of "Hamlet"), long-term dreams (to get a degree in architecture), and really, really long-term dreams (to sail the world in your own handmade boat). Besides your own dreams, you may have dreams for loved ones, your community, and the world. Some of your dreams may be easy to attain; some may seem impossible. You may have one dream, or hundreds!

So dream on! Dreams have no rules: They can't be bought or sold, or bartered. They are born to you, and they belong to you—only you. How you treat them is your decision. You can push them down, hide them away, neglect them until they wither. Or you can lift them up, nourish them, and embrace every place they take you. If you're willing, you can offer your dreams (and yourself!) the greatest gift of all: You can believe in them.

BE YOU...
THEN BE MORE OF YOU!

Writer Gretchen Rubin spent a year studying how to be happy—the theories written about it, the research conducted on it, and the references to it in popular culture through the ages. The result was a book, *The Happiness Project*, and a blog—www.happiness-project.com, and 12 Personal Commandments— the first of which is "Be Gretchen." After all, when you're true to yourself— whoever that self is—happiness is bound to follow!

Name five things you like about yourself. These might range from "I'm a morning person!" to "My passion is to promote literacy among girls all around the world."

1. ....
....
....

2. ....
....
....

3. ....
....
....

4. ....
....
....

5. ....
....
....

Time for Reflection

Have you noticed that dreaming is something you do alone, when you're not busy and distracted, or when you are busy but need an escape? There's a reason for that. Dreaming requires silent reflection. To dream, you first have to tune out the world and tune in to your deepest wishes. There are few better ways to clear your mind than to get outside and exercise—by yourself. Here are some other great ways to dream your best dreams:

* Soak in a hot bath
* Write in a journal
* Lie down and look at the clouds
* Look through old photographs or scrapbooks
* Wander through a museum

Give them a try! And for more great dream starters, look for the "Permission to Dream!" items all along this journey.

If...

Lots of things can come between you and your dreams, including personal fears. If you ever find a fear blocking one of your dreams, shoot it down—out loud: "If I didn't have a fear of public speaking, I might dream of becoming a mayor or governor." Give it a try:

If ....
....
....

I might dream of ....
....
....

Putting Dreams on Paper

Think about your dreams, big, small, wild, simple. Jot them here, in words or images. When you have a good list going, look it over. What patterns do you notice? Are your dreams all short-term or all long-term? All general or all specific? Are they dreams you've had for years, or new dreams you thought up in a snap? As you answer these easy questions, you may gain a deeper understanding of what your dreams say about you.

Have you perhaps had some Girl Scout experiences that have shaped your dreams?

Which of your dreams show you being a leader—in your life, your career, your community?

In the end, your dreams are your story. What kind of story do you want your dreams to tell about you?

DREAM NOW, EDIT LATER

You may not know if a dream is right for you until you give it a chance. Dreaming requires unrestrained imagination. So let your thoughts wander as far as they can go. You might be quick to dismiss a dream if it seems farfetched or silly. But that's like editing a story before you write it!

If you've flown in a plane, you probably remember how the clouds seem billowy and white at first. But then, as you fly through them, they look more like dreary gray fog or rain. Dreams can be the same way. One that sounds amazing from a distance can feel all wrong when you're right in it. And one that you just stumble into can turn out to be ideal for you.

Superstar on Wheels

The first years of **Tatyana McFadden**'s life were spent in an orphanage in St. Petersburg, Russia. Her legs were paralyzed from a condition called *spina bifida*, and she didn't have a wheelchair of her own. So she pulled herself around on her hands, using her arms to support her full weight.

By the time she was adopted, at age 6, Tatyana was severely anemic and had been given just three months to live. Now, Tatyana is not only alive and well, she's a student at the University of Illinois and a six-time Paralympic medalist. And Tatyana, a Girl Scout since she was a young girl, is credited with sparking a new law in Maryland that gives students with disabilities the right to participate side-by-side with their teammates in high school sports.

"Obviously," Tatyana says, matter-of-factly, "there's a purpose to my life."

Her mother, Deborah McFadden, a former commissioner for disabilities at the U.S. Department of Health and Human Services, introduced Tatyana to swimming and then got her involved with a Baltimore, Maryland-based sports program for physically challenged kids. Tatyana tried a number of sports, including what became her two greatest loves: basketball and track. She was a natural at both. At age 15, she competed in the 2004 Paralympic Games in Athens, winning a silver and a bronze medal for track in the 100 meter and 200 meter events, respectively. In 2006, at the IPC (International Paralympic Committee) Athletics World Championships in the Netherlands, she won three medals, including a world-record-time gold in the 100 meter. And in 2008, at the Paralympic Games in Beijing, she brought home four more medals: three silvers, in the 200, 400, and 800 meter events, and a bronze in the 4 x 100 meter relay.

"My motto is, 'Follow your dreams. Anything can happen,'" Tatyana says. "I sort of picked that up at a pretty young age."

But even as Tatyana grabbed headlines for her athletic abilities, she was being denied the right to compete fully in high school track. She raced in her wheelchair, but was timed on her own, alone on the track. She was not allowed to be part of the team. Tatyana filed a lawsuit against the Howard County (Maryland) Board of Education and won. Now a Maryland law requires school districts to allow students with disabilities to be full and equal members of athletic teams and to participate alongside their teammates in all events. Seven more states have since enacted similar laws granting this same access.

"Just being in a wheelchair is a challenge," Tatyana says. But when life throws out an obstacle, "there's always—always—a way around it."

CLIMBING TOWARD A DREAM

Put any 10-month-old baby at the bottom of a flight of stairs, and you're likely to notice the same phenomenon: The baby tries to climb the stairs. At that age, most babies can't even walk, much less manage steps, but their fascination with staircases consistently defies their own abilities. They know what they want, and the idea of attempting to do it is enough to bring them pure, unabashed glee.

Dreams are just like that staircase, and *bliss* is knowing you are exactly where you want to be, doing exactly what you want to be doing. The question isn't whether you will reach the top of those stairs—but when, and how.

GO THERE! Through the Girl Scout *destinations* offerings, you and your group can organize trips to just about anywhere in the world! Search *destinations* at girlscouts.org, and see if you can make a dream come true!

CAREER OPPORTUNITY!

Do you dream of making travel part of your daily life or traveling far and wide? You can! Look into one of these travel-happy careers!

* Pilot
* Flight attendant
* Travel writer
* Tour guide
* International sales agent

VALUES AND STANDARDS: YOUR SPRINGBOARD TO DREAMS

Whether you realize it or not, you live your life by a set of standards. Standards are guidelines, principles, ideals. You've probably adopted your standards without much thought—because, most likely, they're based on your family's values. Those underlying values might include honesty (your parents taught you not to lie or steal) and respect for authority (your parents taught you that, too!). Certainly as you've grown and widened your experiences, you've also adopted values from your schools, your community, and the world.

And now that you're a Girl Scout Ambassador, you've probably started to set some standards of your own. You'll probably adopt many of your family's standards. But you're likely to add some new ones, too—Don't gossip! Eat more protein! Go green! That means you're probably starting to form your own underlying values.

Values and standards don't sound very dreamy, do they? But think about it: How can you dream about ending childhood hunger in your lifetime without valuing health, equity, and the well-being of future generations? And how can you move your dream forward if you don't have your own standards in place about the level of health and well-being that all people should be able to enjoy? And how about your personal standards for achieving this dream? What would they be? What standards will you be an Ambassador for?

GETTING BACK TO VALUES

Look through this list of common values and circle the three that have the most meaning for you in your life right now. This might sound like something you would only do privately, but you probably discuss your values with friends all the time. Think about the last time you ran to a friend's locker after having been called out by a teacher in a class, or when your parents said you couldn't go to Friday night's party but your brother could. Were you talking about fairness, integrity, independence? Those are all values!!

Connection to Community	Teamwork	Stick-to-itiveness
Diversity	Equality	Independence
Fairness	Wisdom	Honesty and Integrity
Kindness	Loyalty	Tolerance
Open-Mindedness	Creative Thinking	Courtesy and Respect

AT THE CORE OF DREAMING

Your values and your standards usually point to what matters to you most. To know your values and standards is to know yourself. And knowing yourself helps you zero in on your dreams. And to zero in on your dreams is to make way for bliss!

TOO TOUGH TO CALL?

Looking over the list, did you find yourself asking, "How do I pinpoint my core values when I value most of these things?" If so, the first question to consider might be: Which of these do I act on the most, and the most naturally— without any hesitation?

Values are inherently positive, and most people like to think of themselves as having mostly positive attributes. So the trick is to prioritize (remember, in the values list, you circled only your top three!), be honest, and try to apply each value to your life. Try this:

1. Take two values at random and pick the one you think is more important. For instance: "Honesty and Integrity" and "Connection to Community." Is it more important to you to stay true to your values and obligations, or to foster a tight relationship with the people around you? Now take the "winner" and compare it to another value. When you find two values of equally high importance in your life, place both on your list of core values and move on to others.

2. Think about what you value in yourself and also what you value in others. You might not think of yourself as particularly good at self-control, but you might highly value self-control in others.

3. Think of a stressful or awkward situation that you recently experienced. Maybe your mom confronted you about alcohol or drug use among your friends, or you got a poor grade on an important test, or a boy you like embarrassed you in the hallway at school. Now think over how you handled it—what do your actions say about your values?

STRIVING FOR VALUES

If you dream of fairness and equality for Earth and all its inhabitants, check out the leadership journey *JUSTICE*. It calls on Ambassadors to devise an equation for environmental justice for all.

The Birth of a Value

Try linking one of your values with a story from your past—maybe you learned the importance of teamwork from playing sports, maybe your grandmother's experience in the military made you admire courage in a whole new way, or maybe you learned about open-mindedness from a favorite teacher.

Your life is filled with stories, each of which has left some imprint on your soul. Tell one of them here, in any form you like—a poem, painting, photo, steps for a dance! Then share it with friends! (Be sure your story expresses the significance it holds for you.)

YOUR CORE REMAINS, EVEN AS YOU CHANGE!

Think about how much you've changed in the last 10 years, or just the last five. If you keep a journal, look back at what you cared about, thought about, and believed. How has it changed? People's outlooks change as they age because they are in different places and stages of life. Where you are right now may be far different from where you'll be six months after you graduate from high school!

Though your core values—kindness, perhaps honesty—will likely stay in place throughout your life, some values—and some dreams, too!—are bound to change or be challenged. That means how you live your life, or carry out your dreams, may change, too.

Girl Scouts' Changing Values

The original Girl Scout Law, established in 1912, was full of values, and most were the same as they are now, although the wording is different. Compare the 1912 version below with the current version on the inside cover of this book. Which value is most important to you? Which way of "saying" that value appeals most to you?

THE GIRL SCOUT LAW OF 1912

A Girl Scout's honor is to be trusted.

A Girl Scout is loyal.

A Girl Scout's duty is to be useful and to help others.

A Girl Scout is a friend to all, and a sister to every other Girl Scout no matter to what social class she may belong.

A Girl Scout is courteous.

A Girl Scout keeps herself pure.

A Girl Scout is a friend to animals.

A Girl Scout obeys orders.

A Girl Scout is cheerful.

A Girl Scout is thrifty.

THE LINES YOU DRAW

Think of standards as the lines you draw for yourself. They can make you different from others or the same as others. Often standards are the difference between yes and no. Every time you begin a sentence with, "It's OK to . . ." or "It's not OK to . . . ," you are setting standards for yourself and for others. Standards can be personal, or they can be laws (It's not OK to drive a car before a certain age) or workplace guidelines (It's not OK to wear jeans at the office).

There are also standards to live up to that are set by others, either individuals, such as your parents (who insist you go to a top college), your friends (who try to insist that you wear what they like), your teachers (who might set high academic standards for you). You could put national health standards in this category. Health standards aren't laws that you have to follow but guidelines recommended for living a long and healthy life. And that means a life with plenty of time for dreams!

TODAY'S DAILY FOOD STANDARDS

At least **3 ounces** of whole-grain bread, cereal, crackers, rice, or pasta

2 cups of vegetables

1½ cups of fruits

3 cups of dairy.
Examples: low-fat milk, cheese, yogurt

5 ounces of protein.
Examples: beef, poultry, nuts, seeds, fish, eggs, beans

5 teaspoons of oils

200 to 400 "discretionary calories."
Examples: high-fat syrups and sauces, sweets, sodas, candy

THE CHANGING PYRAMID

In some ways, national nutritional standards have changed a lot in recent years. Food pyramids constructed by the U.S. Department of Agriculture aim to give people a sense of what to eat, and in what quantities, to maintain a healthy diet. Look at the changes made to the pyramid recently. What foods are valued more today? Notice that physical exercise is now part of the pyramid, too. For teenagers, the standard is to be active for 60 minutes every day, or most days. How does your exercise level rate?

USDA FOOD PYRAMID, 1992

THE CURRENT USDA FOOD PYRAMID

What's Your Story?

Your Pyramid

Have your own health standards kept pace with the USDA's? Do you limit your intake of junk food? Do you exercise for 60 minutes every day? On a scale of 1-10, how satisfied are you with the health standards you now have in your life? If you said 7 or below, challenge yourself! What could you change to improve your health standards?

Track what you eat, and how active you are, for a few days or a week, or even longer, and then make your own health pyramid based on your actual diet and activity level. (If beans are are a slim wedge and donuts are a wide one, you know you've got a problem!) Track your sleep patterns and stress/mood levels, too. By the end of the week, what kind of story do you have to tell? What changes do you want to make? For a fun way to set personal food goals and plan menus based on them, visit www.mypyramidtracker.gov/planner/.

Food   *Exercise*   *Mood*

CAREER OPPORTUNITY!

Did charting your health habits give you a charge of energy? If so, you might consider one of these careers:

* Doctor
* Nurse
* Dietician
* Fitness trainer
* Nutritionist
* Physical therapist
* Health reporter or editor

WHO SETS YOUR STANDARDS FOR BEAUTY?

Beauty is an industry that thrives on the media, and targets girls and women. Why? Because beauty sells. Whether advertisers are selling weight loss, skin care, or hair products—or anything else—the aim is always the same: Make women believe they must have it to be happy, successful, and/or fulfilled. What might happen to a woman's dreams if she always buys into media-driven standards of beauty? What could be done to change her thinking?

If you were a girl whose "parents" were the media, what might you be like? How would you act? What would you believe, and aspire to become? What "look" would you strive for? How would you feel about yourself? Just how different is this Ms. Media from the real you?

*bliss*ful Eats

FROZEN MANGO-BANANA-ORANGE SMOOTHIE

½ cup of frozen mango chunks

1 cup of vanilla yogurt (low-fat or fat-free)

1 banana

½ cup orange juice

4–5 ice cubes

Place all ingredients in a blender and blend until smooth. Then pour into a glass and enjoy!

EMBRACE YOURSELF, EMBRACE YOUR DREAMS!

Have you ever betrayed your standards to match someone else's standards? Maybe you arrived late to a party because you knew most everyone else would, even though you prefer to be on time. Have you ever started a diet even though you look great just because a few of your friends were dieting and you thought you should, too? When you do things that are out of sync with your true you, your body and mind have unmistakable ways of clueing you in, such as:

Insomnia

Feelings of stress

Sweaty palms

Queasiness

Restlessness

Feelings of being conflicted

Anxiety or moodiness

So know who you are and embrace it. In Girl Scouts, that's what is meant by Discovering yourself and your values. Leaders know who they are and what they stand for—and then they stand for it! That's being a leader in your own life (and it will likely get you closer to your dreams, too!). When you are a leader in your own life, you have the best chance of inspiring others around you.

When Double Doesn't Mean More or Better

When you hold different people to different sets of standards, you may be guilty of perpetuating double standards. Many double standards involve men and women. Consider the ones below. What do you think about them? Which ones have you noticed in your own life?

Family: Parents are often more "protective" of daughters and enforce stricter rules on them for curfews, dating, and driving than they do for sons. (Have you noticed this in your life?)

Appearance: In some cultures, women and girls are expected to be thin and youthful, while boys and men are not. (What is the standard in your culture? Do you think you will ever feel pressure to color your hair or turn to plastic surgery to look younger?)

Age: It is routinely accepted that men date women considerably younger than they are. But when women date younger men, they are sometimes mocked or called "cougars," as if they are attacking innocent cubs. (Do you feel that's fair? What name would you give to men who date younger women?)

Career: Despite the passing of the Equal Pay Act, women in the United States today still earn only about 80 cents for every dollar earned by a man doing the same job. (What could you do to ensure that you are paid what you're worth when you enter the workforce?)

For a look at how double standards—and sexism—affected the 2008 presidential election coverage in the United States, check out "Sexism Sells—But We're Not Buying It," a video produced by the Women's Media Center (http://womensmediacenter.com/blog/2008/05/sexism-might-sell-but-were-not-buying-it/).

And while you're at it, take a look at how much sports coverage of women your local news provides, compared to the coverage of men!

News coverage: Sports coverage of male athletes tends to focus on their athletic skills, while stories about elite female athletes often focus on their physical attractiveness. The same is true in politics. Have you ever noticed how the clothing worn by female politicians becomes a topic of discussion, even though it has nothing to do with the stories at hand?

What double standards have you noticed around you? Which ones, if any, are limiting your dreams? Which ones might be limiting the dreams of others? Do your female friends perpetuate any double standards? Do they think you perpetuate any? Ask them!

. . . .

. . . .

. . . .

. . . .

. . . .

Standards for Life

What standards might you set for yourself as you move forward to the next chapter of your life? What story do you want these standards to tell about you? Remember, your standards may become the foundation of your dreams! List some standards you want to adopt. Then try to live by them for a week. Each day, rate yourself (on a scale of 1–5) on how well you stuck to each standard. Try to improve your score each day! Then apply your standards to your dreams! For each standard you named, come up with at least one way that standard will move you toward your dreams, or is doing so already.

Indulge a Little!

A sometimes-treat is sometimes just the thing to get you dreaming! So go ahead and indulge—just once in a while!—with this bliss-ful twist on the classic campfire treat. If indulging, or ice cream, isn't your style, just use all low-fat yogurt and maybe a tablespoon or two of coconut water (it's a potassium-rich superfood!).

SCRUMPTIOUS S'MORE MILKSHAKE

> 3 scoops vanilla ice cream
> ¼ cup low-fat milk
> 1 tablespoon plain, low-fat yogurt
> 12 mini marshmallows
> Graham cracker crumbs for topping
> Chocolate syrup

Toast the marshmallows until they're soft and darkened but not black. Put the ice cream, milk, and yogurt in a blender and blend until you see a hollow core in the center of the shake. Then add 6 of the marshmallows and blend. Pour the mixture into a glass. Top with the remaining marshmallows and the graham cracker crumbs, and a swirl of chocolate syrup.

Valuing Order . . . Seeing Beauty

Even as a young child, landscape architect **Bibi Gaston** valued order. She was a natural-born "straightener." She often studied the dilapidated houses on her way to elementary school in New Jersey and wished they could be fixed or made right. She assumed the people inside were unhappy with their lives.

So she was mortified to find, after the divorce of her parents, that her own house was starting to become rundown. The fence had fallen, and the paint on the outdoor furniture had peeled and chipped. Although little more than 8 years old, Gaston visited a local hardware store, bought items to prevent rust and strip paint, and set to work fixing the furniture and propping up the fallen fence.

Now, some 40 years later, Gaston, who lives near Washington, D.C., is still straightening—in her career as a landscape architect and consultant. She has traveled the world beautifying vacant lots, creating greenery, and planting elaborate gardens. She has created beautiful parks and playgrounds, developed hiking trails, and restored highways. Her most recent project is a massive plant-conservation effort in her native Morocco.

Gaston didn't always see the connection between her values and her dreams, but she does now. "A natural synergy attracted me to places that were really a mess," she says. "Now I'm cleaning up places in the world that are really a mess."

Seeing Real Beauty

Bibi Gaston explored another kind of beauty when she wrote *The Loveliest Woman in America*, a biography about her grandmother, Rosamond Pinchot Gaston. The elder Gaston, a successful actress and model, committed suicide at age 33.

Gaston says the biography gave her a glance into a tragic aspect of society that still exists today: women's obsession with their looks. Her grandmother, who starred in a famous production of "The Miracle" on Broadway, was talented, gorgeous, and a favorite of photographers. Yet when she looked in the mirror, she saw only faults. She would "critique herself," Gaston says. "She said she had a potato nose, and she thought her calves were way too thick. Some days, she would hate herself."

How many friends do you know who are quite good-looking but still think they are flawed? They may be trying to live by someone else's standards of beauty. What sort of story could you tell to change their thinking so that they live by their own standards?

EVERY SONG TELLS A STORY

Every song tells a story, and there are so many songs about dreams. How about writing your own? Start with one word, or one phrase, and see where it takes you. When the band Talking Heads wrote "Dream Operator," they started with this simple phrase: "When you were little, you dreamed you were big." And here is where it led:

Every dream has a name
And names tell your story
This song is your dream
You're the dream operator . . .
And you dreamed it all
And this is your story

CAREER OPPORTUNITY!

Music is a way to bring stories to life. It can also be a path to your dream job. Can you imagine getting paid to work with music every day? Consider these careers:

* Set designer for music videos
* Record label producer
* Web master for music site
* Film scorer
* Music teacher
* Recording engineer
* Band conductor
* Music therapist
* Radio DJ

MUSICAL STANDARDS

What standards do you have for what you listen to, watch, or read?
Do you avoid media that makes you mad, sad, or scared?
Do you avoid music with explicit language or lyrics that talk down
about women? Why or why not?

PERMISSION TO DREAM

Listen to Music

Ever notice how the right music can change your mood in a
(heart)beat?! It's as though the notes are communicating
with a part of your brain that you don't control—and it
may be true! Make a playlist of your favorite songs—
the ones that make you happiest.
Then close your eyes and listen.
See where your mind goes.
Does it go to your
dreams?

THE PURPOSE OF PASSION

Passion is a powerful feeling, a strong desire, an abiding enthusiasm. Passion is the fire in your soul, the energy in your heart. It is the emotion that propels you forward without much need for encouragement or self-discipline. Passion is the spark that all great leaders have. Passion is doing something because, well, you simply must.

Passion may not be necessary to live. But is passion necessary to follow your dreams? Or to be a courageous and inspiring leader? You bet! Without passion, you can't really know your dreams, much less chase them. Passion is to dreaming what a pumping heart is to a body. Without passion, dreams can't survive.

Your Passion Meter

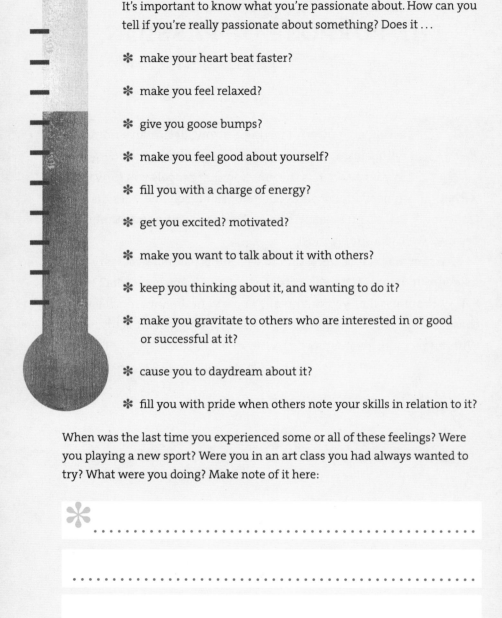

It's important to know what you're passionate about. How can you tell if you're really passionate about something? Does it ...

✳ make your heart beat faster?

✳ make you feel relaxed?

✳ give you goose bumps?

✳ make you feel good about yourself?

✳ fill you with a charge of energy?

✳ get you excited? motivated?

✳ make you want to talk about it with others?

✳ keep you thinking about it, and wanting to do it?

✳ make you gravitate to others who are interested in or good or successful at it?

✳ cause you to daydream about it?

✳ fill you with pride when others note your skills in relation to it?

When was the last time you experienced some or all of these feelings? Were you playing a new sport? Were you in an art class you had always wanted to try? What were you doing? Make note of it here:

✳ ....

....

....

TIPS FOR FINDING YOUR PASSION

If you're not sure what your true passions are, or whether you have any, here are some Do's … and Don'ts:

DO seek out the stories of others—those you know and those you have yet to meet. Ask a parent, grandparent, or guardian what you loved to do as a child and what you were especially good at. A lot of passions begin at a young age and never go away completely. Ask other adults what they do for work and for pleasure. What hobbies do they have? What are their passions? (In the Give It! part of this journey, you'll be talking to women who have been successful in finding their passions and pursuing their dreams. What they tell you may give you some great tips and ideas.)

DO seek out new experiences. Passion must be explored, and explorations require trying new experiences. Every time you open yourself to something new, you invite the possibility of a new passion opening up for you. (Try different workshops, lectures, open houses. They're usually free and informative. Check listings in your area.)

DON'T judge yourself: Being passionate about something doesn't mean you have to be good at it. You might be passionate about fashion but feel all your clothes are unfashionable. You might be passionate about environmentalism but not quite sure what you can do about it.

DON'T let others decide your passion: Passion Busters are people who downplay, or even quash, the passion of those around them. Passion Busters might discourage you, or make you feel guilty. But they have no real power over you—unless you give it to them.

POWERED BY PASSION

Are you passionate about an issue and want to make sure your message gets heard? Check out *Your Voice, Your World: The Power of Advocacy*. This Girl Scout leadership journey invites Ambassadors like you to speak up and speak out for positive change.

Healthy Passions

Eating right and exercising can feel an awful lot like work when you're not enjoying the food or the sweat. But when you find foods and exercise you're passionate about, there's not a lick of work involved! So, if you're trying to eat better, research other cuisines to find ideas for healthful dishes you'll like. And if you want to exercise more, find a physical activity that you can be passionate about! You might just surprise yourself, and please your body, when you learn that you adore salted seaweed and are crazy about break dancing before breakfast! Use this space to share the story of one of your healthy passions:

How to Spot a Passion Buster:

* You don't speak up or act like yourself around this person.
* The person makes you feel less confident in your abilities.
* You feel your dreams aren't being taken seriously, or respected.

How to Stop a Passion Buster:

* Be true to yourself and your passions. Always act like yourself, and ask that your dreams be taken seriously.
* Demonstrate that you take your dreams seriously, and be unapologetic about following them.

PERMISSION TO DREAM

Make Something!

Doing something creative—whether singing a song, canning homemade pickles, or choreographing a dance step—offers one of the most direct routes to your innermost self. When you do something you love, you put yourself in the perfect frame of mind for dreaming. So, for starters, set aside 30 minutes a day to devote to something purely creative.

You may not know exactly what you want to do with those 30 minutes, so try whatever comes to mind! You might develop your own recipe for a new dinner salad, one you can share with your whole family. Or you might turn on the radio to a random station and dance your heart out to whatever's playing. Or you might grab a notebook, go outside, and sit under the nearest tree and see where your imagination takes you! Did the 30 minutes really seem like 10? If your answer was yes, you picked a true passion. How about devoting 40 minutes to that passion next week? See how it goes! A creative break can make you even better at all those other important things in life—family, school, work, and exercise!

REACH FOR THE CLOUDS
MOBILE

A dream mobile with clouds, rainbows, the sun and planets, and other symbols is just the thing to keep you dreaming. And it's another creative break that will lift your head into the clouds. You can keep it in your room, your locker, anywhere it will inspire you. After you make one for yourself, consider making another with or for a younger dreamer in your family or circle. She can literally reach for the clouds, too! It's fun and easy, and you can use materials you have around the house. Here's what you need:

One curtain ring or other lightweight ring, such as the rim from an oatmeal container

Lightweight cardboard

Hole punch

Cotton or cotton balls, fabric scraps, ribbon, braid, colored markers or paint to decorate with

Nylon fishing line, heavy thread, or yarn

Pencil

Draw clouds or other shapes on the cardboard, cut out the shapes, and decorate as desired, keeping all the shapes about equal in weight. Punch a hole at the top of each. Cut the fishing line, thread, or yarn into various lengths, thread them through the holes on the decorated shapes, and tie. Tie the other ends around the ring so the shapes hang below the ring in a pleasing, balanced arrangement. Next cut four equal lengths of the fishing line, and tie one end of each to the ring at the 12, 3, 6, and 9 o'clock positions. Bring the loose ends of the line together at the top of the ring, and secure them together with a knot. Use the knotted end to suspend the mobile.

CONNECTING YOUR VALUES
TO YOUR PASSIONS,
AND A PASSION TO DREAMS

Building dreams starts by focusing on your passions. You've been exploring passions, values, and standards. What dreams do they lead you to? Now's the time to find out. Using the columns below, jot down some of your passions. Then name the values behind those passions. Next, try connecting each passion to possible dreams, using the chart below. Remember, no dream is too big! So as you dream big, dream as wide as possible, too: Think of all the various ways your passions can become dreams.

Passion	Value	Dream I	Dream II	Dream III
I love to garden	Green lifestyle	Plant my own garden	Own a nursery	Become a landscape architect
I am enamored with filmmaking	Creativity	Learn how to edit home movies using computer software	Studyscreenwriting after high school, so I can work in the film industry	

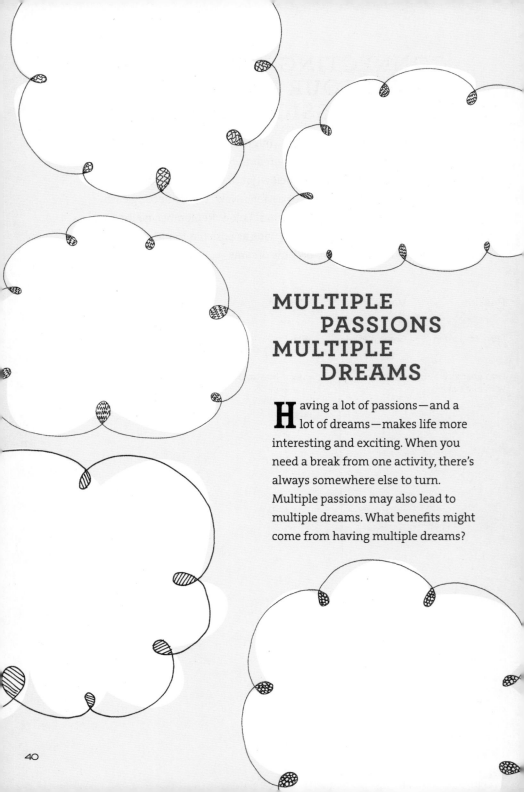

MULTIPLE PASSIONS MULTIPLE DREAMS

Having a lot of passions—and a lot of dreams—makes life more interesting and exciting. When you need a break from one activity, there's always somewhere else to turn. Multiple passions may also lead to multiple dreams. What benefits might come from having multiple dreams?

DON'T FORGET YOUR STANDARDS!

Once you've got some big dream ideas going, it's easy to see how your standards enable you to move your dreams forward. For example, if your dream is become a landscape architect, then your standards for education, for beauty in nature, and for environmental stewardship may all be key to your moving forward on this dream path.

CAREER OPPORTUNITY!

Charity needn't be just an occasional activity in your life. If you're passionate about giving, "work" it into your career!

For example, any position with a nonprofit organization, from chief executive on down, could bring you bliss! Just choose one that makes the best use of your skills and interests! Like to sell? Raise funds? Design graphics? Do that for an organization whose mission speaks to you!

PERMISSION TO DREAM

Volunteer!

Sometimes you have to step outside yourself for a while to see what really matters to you. Volunteering, whether for a homeless shelter, a fund-raiser, or any other cause that strikes your heart, may be just the ticket. Giving something of yourself to others creates inner peace— just the sort of environment dreams need to take root.

2 Passions
+1 Groundbreaking Career
= Realized Dream
(aka Bliss)

Growing up in Brooklyn, New York, **Irene Pepperberg** had two abiding passions: birds and science. Her interest in birds began as a young child, when her parents brought home a parakeet to keep her company. It was the first of many parakeets she would own, love, and teach to talk. Her interest in science came later, in school, when she realized that she grasped scientific concepts almost effortlessly and was fascinated by the periodic table of chemical elements.

When the time came to choose a career path, Pepperberg chose chemistry. She graduated from the Massachusetts Institute of Technology and went on to receive her master's in chemistry from Harvard University. She was so gifted that Harvard accepted her into its Ph.D. program in chemical physics.

Pepperberg was on track to become a physicist. But while working on her doctorate, she realized that something was missing. Although she was following one of her passions— science—the work wasn't as fulfilling as she thought it would be. One day, she saw a TV program about language cognition in dolphins and other

animals. Suddenly, she knew what was missing from her life's work: birds.

So when she finished her doctorate, Pepperberg made the brave decision to switch gears and move into behavioral science. She opened her own lab and spent the next three decades working with an African Grey Parrot named Alex. Her goal was to determine whether parrots have the ability to understand language, not just mimic speech.

"I love doing research," says Pepperberg, now a lecturer at Harvard and an adjunct associate professor at Brandeis University. "I love working with the birds. I love trying to figure out what they know and how they know it." Pepperberg had found a perfect way to meld her two childhood passions.

She found that Alex could reason on a basic level and use words creatively— far exceeding previous assumptions about bird intelligence. The work was mind-boggling to a world that still used the term "bird brain" as an insult.

Pepperberg is credited with changing the way people think about birds. There are few greater thrills than making scientific leaps that have never been made before, she says. "When you do something that works . . . you have discovered something that no one else in the world knows, based on your abilities," she says. "It's an amazing feeling to have that knowledge."

What's Your Story?

Childhood Passions, Lifelong Dreams

Chances are good that some of your greatest passions are also some of your oldest. What did you love to do as a kid? What brought you the most joy? Were you athletic? Did you love books? Were you always inspecting bugs or flowers, staring at the stars, putting on shows?

Think back on all the things you chose to do when you were care-free and creative. Which of your past passions have you carried with you into your current life? Which ones have you lost along the way? Which do you want to bring back? Get them back and infuse some new life into them!

WHAT EVERY DREAMER NEEDS

Say you want to play in the WNBA, become a prima ballerina, cure cancer, and join a space mission to Mars. You can dream it all, but can you really have it all? Achieving dreams isn't a science. And there is no algorithm for determining a dream's achievability. In fact, some of the greatest dreams ever accomplished were those that seemed unattainable.

Which of your dreams will become part of your life story depends on you. But no matter what your dream, to achieve it you need to be a leader in your own life. In Girl Scouts, the Discover Key to leadership calls on you to take challenges, and the best leaders approach challenges with:

* **Determination:** Stick-to-itiveness is not just valuable; it's crucial!

* **Flexibility:** Circumstances change. You change. Be open-minded and switch gears when you need to, even if it means changing gears and trying something new—from the ways you stay focused to the actual details of your dream.

* **Mastery:** Taking a skill to the highest level possible.

Are determination, flexibility, and mastery already among your values and standards? If not, adopt them!

MASTERY IN THREE STEPS

Mastering a skill—whether sinking a free-throw shot, using the latest electronic gadget, or speaking a new language—comes down to three steps.

1. Practice.

2. Practice.

3. Practice.

It takes time to master any dream-worthy skill! That's why a dream based on what you're really passionate about is the best kind of dream. After all, you're going to spend a lot of time on it, so you really want to enjoy what you're doing.

MASTER GIRL SCOUT: JULIETTE GORDON LOW

Juliette "Daisy" Gordon Low made mastery a Girl Scout tradition. Since the organization's start in 1912, leadership has been about mastering practical skills—from camping and first-aid to artistic endeavors and financial literacy and advocacy. In fact, Low considered the earning of a Girl Scout badge to symbolize mastery of a particular concept or skill. How many concepts or skills have *you* mastered as a Girl Scout?

Your Handbag of Skills

Life is not about having one set of skills, or one way forward. You likely have countless skills that you take for granted! Think about all your skills, those that grew from personal interests, from an experience, or a person, place, or issue—anything from your ability to sell a box of cookies to your ability to advocate for a cause you care about. What skills do you have? Which do you want to grow further? What new skills do you want to learn? What sort of story do you want your handbag of skills to tell?

TIPS FOR MAKING MASTERY A PART OF YOUR LIFE

Life is busy. What with school, part-time jobs, friendships, and other obligations, you can easily get sidetracked from your dreams. So, to stay on track with achieving your dreams, make sure you take time to be . . .

Deliberate:
Schedule the time you need to master whatever it is you want to master.

Strategic:
Find ways to weave practice time into what's already happening in your life.

Flexible:
If you can't make your scheduled practice time on a particular day, change it.

Forgiving:
When you don't meet all your goals, go easy on yourself. (But if your practice time keeps getting bumped, see **Be flexible** at left.)

STICKING TO IT . . . OR NOT?

Even the most passionate people run out of steam now and then. That's OK. Running out of steam can signal that you just need a break! But if you want to keep your energy going, here are some tips for staying revved up even when your dreams take a few turns (even sharp left turns or U-turns!) along the way:

* Rather than focusing on end goals, set smaller, mini-goals that work toward your larger goal.

* Write your goals in a visible place and read them regularly.

* Be realistic about your expectations and your timeline for achieving goals.

* Seek out role models who inspire you, and learn what you can from them about their stick-to-it strategies.

* Cut yourself slack, and take breaks to get re-inspired. (Make use of all the Permission to Dream suggestions in this journey!)

* And keep in mind that any turns you take can teach you something you might not have learned any other way! You may even take what you've learned and apply it to other aspects of your life—perhaps even another dream!

blissful Eats

CLOUDBERRY JAM

Cloudberries are small golden berries native to Sweden. If you can find cloudberry jam in your area, try it on waffles, or over frozen yogurt!

Mastering Technology in the Name of Art

In some ways, **Mouna Andraos** invents her dreams. The tech-savvy artist dismantles everyday electronic gadgets, rethinks their shapes and functions, and turns them into useful (and very cool) works of art.

A native of Beirut now based in Montreal, Canada, Andraos has created everything from stand-alone nightlights (made of rubber-encased LEDs and conductive thread) and digital clocks (which she reinvents by juxtaposing clock circuitry with 17th-century French textile prints) to an umbrella-topped mobile unit called the Power Cart that delivers alternative energy to people out on the street.

Some of Andraos' funkiest creations are wearable. In addition to a scarf with a built-in MP3 player, Andraos has created "Solargold," a piece of jewelry

built around a solar panel, and "Address," a necklace pendant she created with fellow artist Sonali Sridhar, which is fitted with a GPS device so you always know exactly how far you are from home—or any place you consider home. "It's something that you could wear close to your heart, and could be an emotional link ... with a special place in the world," Andraos says. Andraos' work reflects her desire to "warm up" technology, to give it a feminine touch.

"Part of the work is trying to say, 'Let's re-imagine electronics.' These things are becoming more and more important in our lives. Can we have a wider conversation about how they look, how they function, what they do?"

Andraos has a graduate degree in interactive communications and also

"Solargold" by Mouna Andraos

works as a Web site designer, a job she loves. Staying on top of the latest technology is a constant challenge, but it's essential to her art, she says. "Technology—how things work—is like my paint," she says. "I need to master it to do the work I do."

Not everyone possesses the head of an engineer and the heart of an artist. But for Andraos, and others like her, the field of tech-art may just be a dream come true.

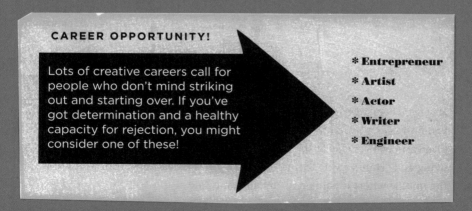

CAREER OPPORTUNITY!

Lots of creative careers call for people who don't mind striking out and starting over. If you've got determination and a healthy capacity for rejection, you might consider one of these!

* **Entrepreneur**
* **Artist**
* **Actor**
* **Writer**
* **Engineer**

WHAT YOU LOVE
+ WHAT YOU LEARN TO MASTER
= DREAM POSSIBILITIES

Your *bliss* may not be wrapped up in having a particular career, but the work you choose can be a starting point for living your dreams. And, let's face it: Whether you live to work or work to live, it's always best to love what you do. So spend your time well!

WHAT I DO WELL
excel in honors biology class

WHAT I LOVE
snorkeling to see underwater sea life, traveling to tropical climates

WHERE DREAMS COME TRUE
becoming a marine biologist doing underwater research around the world

WORK
volunteer: tour guide at aquarium; after school job: taking orders at local burger joint; summer job: lifeguard at the beach

Have you ever loved something you weren't necessarily skilled at doing? Have you ever been skilled at something you didn't necessarily love? Have you ever loved and were skilled at something but realized there was no way to make a living at it? Here's a way to find the overlap, if there is any yet—that place in the middle where dreams can, and do, come true.

Draw some clouds for yourself and fill them in to see if you can find what you have, don't have, and need to do!

What Dream Job Might Be in Your Future?

What did your cloud mapping tell you about your "dream job" that you didn't already know?

WHEN A ROADBLOCK OPENS UP A NEW DREAM

No matter what your dream, you are bound to hit a roadblock now and then. Roadblocks needn't make you give up on a dream. In fact, as you maneuver around them, you may just find that they lead you to an even better dream. Read on!

Finding a True Dream While Longing for Another

Annie Weisman Macomber loved going to plays with her parents when she was growing up in San Diego. Watching the actors made her want to run up onstage to sing and dance and be a star. But when she auditioned for roles, she ended up being cast in the chorus—she felt like she was simply background music for the main show!

"I thought, 'Oh, they don't know what I can do ... If only I was up there, I would be great,'" Annie says.

For months, she persevered. But the more she auditioned, the more disappointed she became. Rarely was she offered more than a small part.

The turning point came in high school. Annie's teachers encouraged her to writes scenes for plays, to create characters that seemed real to her. She found she had a talent for giving her characters dialogue that sounded playful, funny, and even poetic.

When she watched the actors perform her scenes, she realized writing was where her true passion lay.

"That was a big light bulb for me," she says. "I thought, 'Oh, no, no, no! What I want to do is be behind the scenes. I want to write.'"

And so she did. Her plays, "Be Aggressive," about high-school cheerleaders, and "Hold Please," about younger and older women who work in an office, are performed in theaters around the country. She's gone on to write for television and cable TV shows, such as "Eastwick," "Samantha Who?" and "Heartland." And she still writes plays. Her play "Lifted," about a teenager who works at a store and is tempted to steal, was performed at dozens of middle schools and high schools.

Even though she has a successful career as a writer, she's happy that she tried so hard to become an actor. "I had to do all of that. You have to try that out and have that experience, and fail," she says. Her failures helped her realize where she truly fit.

"Ideally when something feels right, it should feel like freedom," Annie says, "whereas sometimes you try different things, and it feel restrictive. You feel like you're trying to be someone else. When it's right for you, you should have the feeling of freedom and open space."

NO DREAM YET? NO WORRIES!

Annie Weisman Macomber was unusual—by high school, she knew exactly what she wanted to do. But it's often good to take a while to decide what you really want to do with your life. You don't need to decide your future by age 17! And there isn't necessarily just one direction for you to take. Take a look back at all the Tips for Finding Your Passion on page 35. And review the chart, page 39, for Connecting Your Values to Your Passions, and a Passion to Dreams. When you find your passion, your career path may follow right behind!

DREAMING FOR ME

Your dreams may change and evolve over time as you move forward in your life. You don't necessarily know what dreams you want to achieve but you can still start to set the scene for your future. And as your dreams come into focus, they will continue to shape the larger story of your life.

So imagine yourself at 100 years old. Think about where you're living, what your home looks like, what you're wearing.

What do you consider your proudest moments in life?

How many of your goals have you achieved?

What are you most passionate about doing now?

Now, get started stepping yourself toward this dream life of yours! Your options are many. After all, various paths might lead you to your dreams.

For many, the natural route to a satisfying (and blissful!) life is a meandering trail, or a zigzag with switchbacks. Some people might detour along the way and dabble here and there before reaching their destination. A meandering path sometimes lands people where they never intended. But that place often ends up being better than they could ever have imagined!

Other people make a beeline from dream planning to dream achievement. They take all the required courses in high school, get a specific degree in their chosen field, land the perfect internship, and get an entry-level job and work their way up the ladder.

Whatever your approach, there are no wrong turns. So take time to smell the roses: Let yourself enjoy some bliss all along the way! Every step gets you closer to where you're going. And a blissful bonus is that you'll be . . .

* *learning from your experience*
* *acquiring valuable skills to carry with you for life*
* *focusing in on what you really want*
* *expanding your network*

PERMISSION TO DREAM
Visit a Cemetery!

If you've been to Paris, you probably know how popular—and peaceful—cemeteries are on a sunny afternoon. (Never been? Visit www.girlscouts.org/destinations.) Headstones are poignant reminders of life stories played out through the ages. In Paris, those life stories include more than a few world-renowned artists, writers, and musicians!

Visit a cemetery near you to see what stories you can find. Check out the types of headstones and what's written on them. What would you like your own epitaph to be? What would it say about you and your dreams?

YOUR MISSION,
YOUR LIFE, YOUR STORY

Girl Scouting builds girls of courage, confidence, and character who make the world a better place.

Sound familiar? That's because it's the mission statement of the Girl Scouts. Mission statements highlight what an organization or company stands for and what it aspires to be. Look up some of the mission statements for your favorite brands. What do they say? Do they speak to you?

You can benefit from writing a mission statement, too! A mission statement gives you the opportunity to state who you are, what's important to you, and where you want to go—all in one neat story line. Being tuned in to their own personal mission is something all leaders aim for! They Discover themselves and their values and then rely on those values as they Connect with others and Take Action in the world.

So write a short mission statement for living your bliss. Draw on all that you have explored along this journey— your values, standards, and passions—to identify what you stand for and what you aspire to be. No need to make the writing perfect. Just focus on capturing a set of ideas that represent you. You can revisit and revise anytime. And remember: You are an Ambassador for the Girl Scout mission! How does that shape your BLISS mission?

My Mission Statement:

SPREAD
THE *BLISS*

Try this with friends! Think we're kidding? We're not! A personal mission is worth wearing on your sleeve. So be proud of it and share it around with friends and family. Who knows? You might inspire others to create their own mission statements, too!

Reward Yourself!

Each time you accomplish a goal or
task, reward yourself. You deserve it!
Take a glorious hike as a study break.
Savor a delicious dessert. Pamper
yourself with a manicure. The
reward need only strike your fancy,
rejuvenate you, and inspire
even more results!

bliss
Give It!

WANTED: DREAM-MAKERS

Your dreams are likely rich and plentiful. Your mind teems with all the exciting things you'd like to do and accomplish. You're not alone: Every woman you know or meet likely has equally vibrant dreams.

That's where this part of the **bliss** journey is headed. *BLISS: Give It!* takes you into the world around you—into the dreams of others. It asks that you use your strengths and passions to support and nurture those dreams. Encouraging the dreams of others—cheering on their aspirations and moving them forward—not only gives others bliss, it gives you some, too.

The bliss of giving to others and assisting others—that's exactly what all leaders experience as they strengthen themselves and lift up those around them!

To give bliss is to live bliss. Bliss and **bliss**—see how they both flip?

BOOST A DREAM, EARN AN AWARD!

On this *bliss* journey, you have the opportunity to earn the prestigious Dream Maker Award. The steps to this leadership award have you identifying a dream that needs help moving forward and getting the dreamer started on a plan to achieve it.

You might help someone create a dream from the bottom up. You might shape a dream that's already partially started. You might save a dream that was nearly lost. You might even boost a dream into reality.

As you move your "adopted dream" forward, you'll connect with dreamers in your community and, if possible, the wider world. Just think how your network of dreamers will grow!

You can work toward the Dream Maker Award on your own or with a team (large or small) of sister Ambassadors. The choice is up to you! Either way, what you do will be important, and your results will be inspiring!

To earn the Dream Maker Award, you have four steps to follow, all of which draw on your own values, standards, creativity, skills, and talent—and dreams! You'll find that each step has a whole journey section devoted to it!

You might...

create a dream from the bottom up . . . You might find a mother of toddlers in your neighborhood who never realized that her skill and passion for putting together her own necklaces could lead to a home-based jewelry business that would let her earn money while being a stay-at-home mom.

shape a dream that's partially started . . . You might help a star teen athlete move toward a career as a pro soccer player.

save a dream that was nearly lost . . . You might help a corporate executive who has wandered away from her true passion of drawing find her way back to being an artist.

boost a dream into reality . . . you might help an older woman who works as a clerk at your grocery store finally realize her dream of earning a college degree!

GOING FOR GOLD?

Taking a journey and earning its award is a first step toward going for the Girl Scout Gold Award, the highest award in Girl Scouting (check it out at www.girlscouts.org). Moving a dream forward on this *bliss* journey gives you valuable networking and planning skills and experience you can draw on for a Girl Scout Gold Award project. The Dream Maker Award moves you up the Girl Scout leadership ladder to reach for the clouds! Now, that sounds dreamy, doesn't it?

1. MEET SUCCESSFUL DREAMERS

Find and then interview three successful women in your community about their dreams and how they have pursued and/or achieved them. (This will show you the path to a successful dream and how dreams get moved forward, even in small ways!)

2. SEEK AND SELECT A DREAMER (OR DREAMERS)

Identify a woman or girl (or a group of women and/or girls) who would benefit from your assistance in realizing a dream and who welcomes your assistance.

3. DEFINE THE DREAM

Together you and the dreamer(s) draft a mission statement that clearly sets out the dream. Then you draw up the steps that will move the dream forward. Coming up with the correct steps will involve a little research! (A mission statement will give the dream vision and focus. Planning out the steps to the dream makes the dream tangible—if you get stuck or a step seems too big, return to the plan! You might have to step it out more, or you may have to change some steps altogether!)

4. GIVE IT! GIFT IT!

Help your dreamer(s) take a step forward in the dream plan, and gift the set of steps for the dream to her. (Taking a step forward will energize your dreamer(s) and start the momentum that will keep the dream progressing! When you are ready to gift the plan, consider making a ceremony of it, perhaps at the journey's closing celebration. The plan may serve as a symbolic remembrance of your collaboration on this dream!)

FROM SAMPLE TO REAL LIFE

The project examples throughout these pages show how to step out specific dream plans. Let these examples inspire you to feel the bliss by helping someone find their dream!

The examples will help you zero in on a dreamer you want to assist, and they'll help you find the best way to move your dreamer(s) forward.

Just remember: Dreams and dreamers can be found almost anywhere. And they can be any age. But be sure the dream you choose to move forward is "dream worthy":

THE DREAM MAKER AWARD IS ABOUT ACHIEVING SOMETHING SIGNIFICANT AND LASTING FOR OTHERS AND FOR YOURSELF! THE REAL REWARD HERE IS THE BLISS YOU'LL BOTH FEEL!

So, a dream headed toward bliss is not about...

❋ **money or material gain . . .**
   if financial resources are blocking your dreamer's dream, find another way around the situation. Instead of taking an expensive writing class, could your dreamer gain experience through an internship at a magazine? Could she barter her time or talents to cover the cost of an expensive cooking class?

❋ **or helping your family or someone you already know well . . .**

The Dream Maker Award is about expanding your network and your reach and gaining experience that will help inform your own dreams, too! So, search for a dreamer who will expand and enrich your story (that's something worth doing throughout life!).

Think adults with careers don't need your help? Think aga Think younger kids don't dream? You're wrong! You and you sister Ambassadors might even choose help girls your own age—those who dre big but don't yet kn how to get there.

Keep in mind that y role on this journey to educate and insp others toward bliss!

MEET SUCCESSFUL DREAMERS

People's dreams may differ widely, but the sentiment behind most dreams is strikingly similar. Most people—regardless of their age, status, experience, religion, heritage, or culture—dream of achieving something bigger and better, for themselves and others.

In the years before Juliette Gordon Low founded the Girl Scouts, she, too, was searching for something important to do with her life. She wanted to accomplish something bigger than herself, something that would benefit others and improve the world around her. Her determination and vision led her to fulfill her dream.

NETWORKING FOR DREAM STORIES

How do you find out about the dreams of others? Network! Talking about dreams with others can be a great way to deepen your relationships with people—and a great way to explore all the types of dreams that exist in the world. It's also a great way to find a dream to adopt. Spread the word among your friends (and friends of friends!) that you're on a quest to collect dream stories, that you want to know their biggest and wildest dreams, and their smallest, too. See what they say.

Take your dream quest to parties, school events, and family get-togethers—use it as an ice breaker. See what dream stories you uncover! If you're going for the Dream Maker Award, there's no better way to prepare for supporting someone else's dream than by exploring the whole range of dreams being dreamed in the world—the more dreams you learn about, the better equipped you'll be to help your adopted dreamer(s)!

For every dream you collect on your quest, fill in one dream cloud. Keep going until each cloud is filled. Then consider these questions:

What connections do you feel to these dreams you've collected?

How does thinking about these dreams bring you closer to your own dreams?

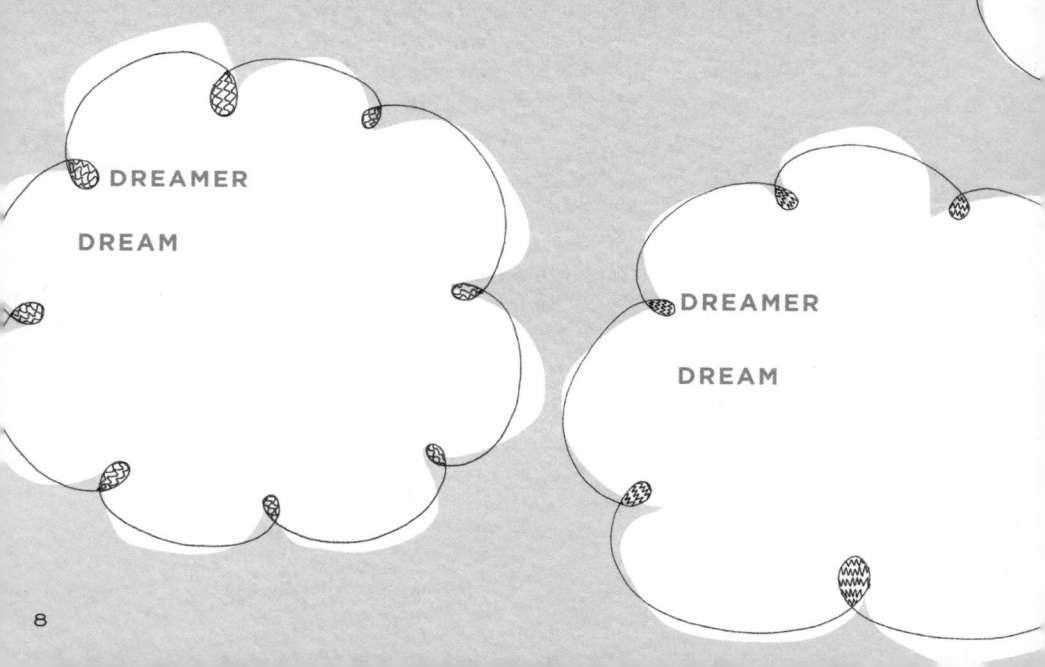

DREAMER

DREAM

DREAMER

DREAM

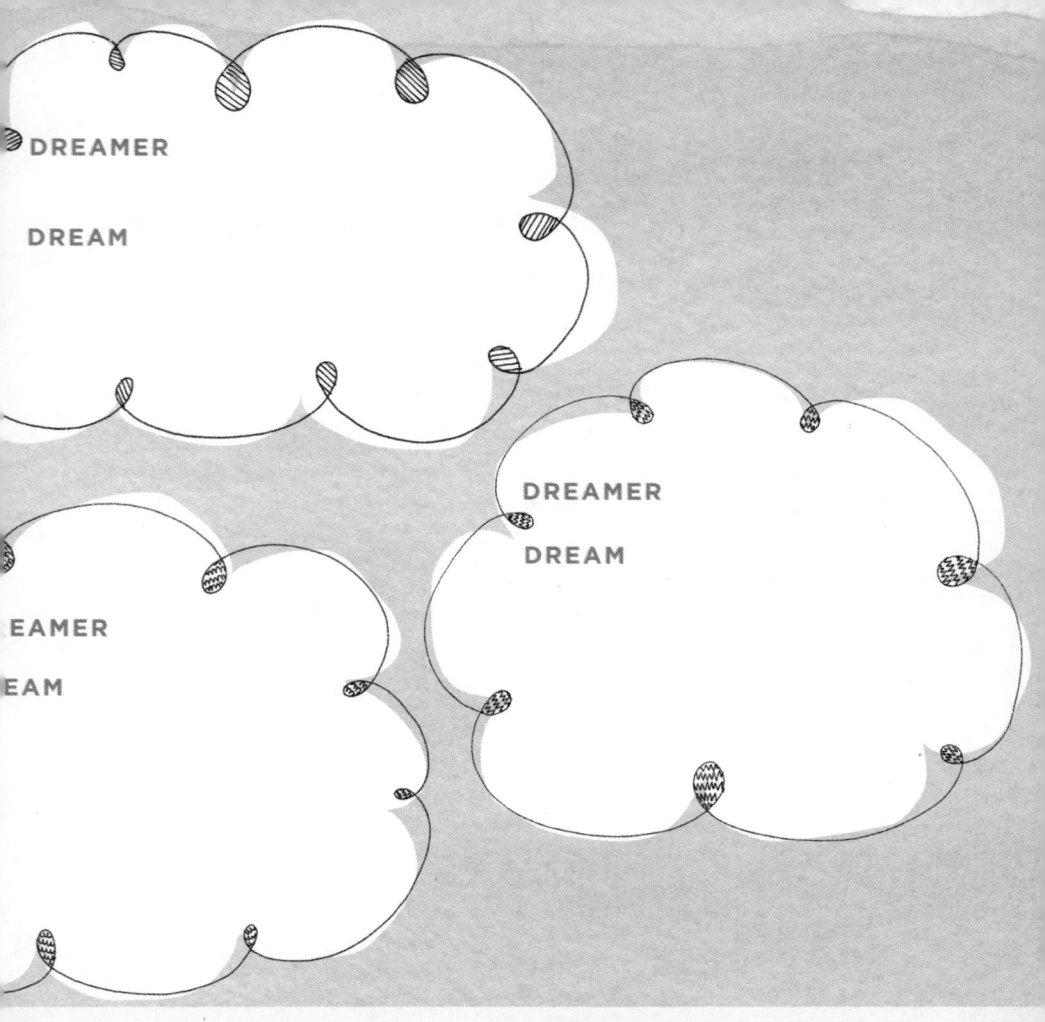

DREAMER

DREAM

DREAMER

DREAM

EAMER

EAM

YOUR SYMBOL OF BLISS

Sketch a symbol that captures your hopes for the world—
and all its dreamers! Share it when your Ambassador team gets together!

READY, SET, GO!
THE INTERVIEW PROCESS

There are few better ways to get to know someone—and their dreams—than to interview them.

Step 1 of the Dream Maker award calls on you (on your own or with your sister Ambassadors) to interview three women about their dreams and how they achieved them or are reaching toward them. Exploring the ways these women identified and live their dreams (or continue to work toward them) will help you approach your own dreams and help plan out the dreams of others.

So, who to interview? Word-of-mouth is a good way to find interview candidates! Ask around. You're sure to learn of women likely to spark your interest and inspire you—perhaps a city council member, a yoga teacher, or the entrepreneurial mother of a friend, or a family member's business partner.

COMFORT (AND SAFETY) IN NUMBERS!

When interviewing people you don't know, hold the interview in a public place, like a coffee shop or a meeting room at your local library. If you and your sister Ambassadors are working toward the Dream Maker Award together, consider inviting your dreamers to an Ambassador gathering for a group interview session.

If you're interviewing on your own and you want to stay safe and feel more comfortable, bring along a friend, who can either sit in on the interview or simply wait for you till it ends. And be sure to tell your family and friends where you are and what you're doing—it's a smart thing to do no matter what your age.

If you must interview dreamers via e-mail, don't share any personal information that you would not share with strangers.

UNDERSTANDING VALUES, UNDERSTANDING PEOPLE

When you're trying to get to know someone better, either through an interview or anytime in life, it helps to understand their values. Values aren't always easy to spot! To understand the values of others, pay attention to:

• How they spend their time
• What they talk about
• How they act
• What they read
• What they like to do

There's no doubt that shared values bring people together.

Setting the Scene

There's a time and place for everything. Asking people if you can interview them takes a little finesse and good timing. Ensure a successful interview by choosing ...

✳ someone who is neither rushed nor preoccupied. Someone who has time to sit with you and focus on your questions will give you the best interview.

✳ a comfortable place for the interview. Coffee shops, park benches, and quiet living rooms are great interview settings.

✳ someone who is upbeat about life. If someone is going through a difficult personal time—a breakup or a family problem—it may be best to hold off on the interview until things look up.

APPLY THIS TO MEETING NEW PEOPLE . . .

Meeting people—and getting to know them—can be a tricky. The next time you meet someone you think you might be interested in really knowing, or even dating, try these tips!

. . . AND JOB INTERVIEWS, TOO!

Job interviewers aren't the only ones who get to ask questions. Whether you're applying for a job, a volunteer position, or a summer internship, come with your own questions! Not only will you get more out of the process, but you'll impress your potential bosses with your initiative.

"Be Prepared!"

This famous Girl Scout motto can be applied in just about any situation—including this one! Interviews turn out best when you've prepared a few key questions in advance. You'll want to be sure to ask your successful dreamers questions that let you learn about their passions and their values and how the two work together. As you meet with each dreamer, be sure to really listen to what she's saying. When something sparks a new question, just go with the flow! Here are some questions to get you started, and space to add your own!

You really seem to have a dream job (or a truly enriching way to spend free time). Do you see it that way?

What challenges have you faced? How did you get past them?

Who helped you? What did they do?

What got yo started in yo career (or ho or passion)

What were the steps along the way, big or small, that moved your dream forward?

What advice would you give others about following a dream like yours?

What value keep you goi now?

What values got you into this project/ job/passion?

Was there ever a time that you doubted the path you were on? (If yes: What kept you going?)

Do you have eve more dreams fo yourself? (If yes: What wi you tackle next

OTHER TIPS FOR A GREAT INTERVIEW

✳ Ask open-ended questions—questions that can't be answered with a "yes" or "no."

✳ Encourage the person to talk by listening with interest and giving feedback when appropriate.

✳ Feel free to talk about your own dreams. Sharing things about yourself can put your interviewee at ease and let her know this is supposed to be fun!

NOW GO OUT AND INTERVIEW!

DREAMER INTERVIEWED	DATE	DREAM Being lived or worked toward	INSIGHTS LEARNED ABOUT • Finding a Dream • Pursuing a Dream . . . • Persevering with a Dream

YOUR "RESEARCH" WILL COME IN HANDY!

Interviews of successful dreamers are bound to turn up great tips for moving a dream forward. Some of what you learn may even parallel the "Tips for Making Mastery a Part of Your Life" on page 48 of the Live It! side of this journey. So keep your ears tuned for these strategies, which you can use for your dreamer and elsewhere in your own life. That's exactly what great leaders do—they take the best of what they learn and apply it wherever they can.

HELPING AN ARTIST RECOGNIZE HER DREAM AND MOVE IT FORWARD

An Ambassador who loves art decides to help an aspiring artist. She asks all her teachers at school for their ideas about dreamers they may know in the arts. A Spanish teacher mentions her former colleague, a retired French teacher who has been an avid photographer on the side for decades.

The Ambassador contacts Mira, 60, and learns that she has been taking pictures of her home region—the Gulf Coast—her entire life. In talking with her, Mira realizes how wonderful it would be to share her latest series of photos—of the aftermath of Hurricane Katrina—with a public audience.

STEPS OF THE DREAM PLAN:

The Ambassador meets with Mira to learn about her and her work, and to start working with her on a mission statement that clearly sets out her dream of sharing these photos with the public. They settle on this mission statement: *My dream is to put my photographs of the Katrina-ravaged Gulf Coast on wide public display so others can see how the spirit of the people has endured, and how the place is now returning to its former glory.*

WHERE TO SHOW THE PHOTOS?

Then the Ambassador and Mira brainstorm and research ways to get her photographs seen in their area. The Ambassador loves going to art events and has seen a flier for an upcoming open-studio day, when artists open up their work space to the public to show and talk about their work. Mira has never thought of herself as an artist, and is initially reluctant to take part. The Ambassador encourages her to apply. When Mira is accepted, the Ambassador volunteers to work with her to organize the photographs and help with any crowd control needs on the big day.

PREPARING FOR OPEN STUDIO DAY

Mira has taken hundreds of photos through the years. As she sifts through her work, the Ambassador realizes that Mira has lots of portraits of the people. What's more, the Ambassador learns that Mira took detailed notes of the conversations she had with those people, and even made audio recordings of some of them.

WHAT ELSE THE DREAMER IS INSPIRED TO DO

The Ambassador is so fascinated by the stories that Mira tells about the people in her photos that she encourages Mira to incorporate them into her artwork. Mira is inspired to work with a local audio engineer to make digital recordings of the stories.

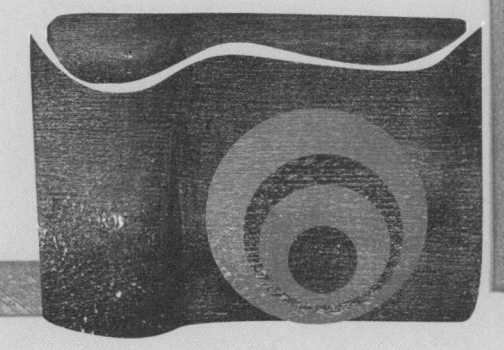

SEEK AND SELECT A DREAMER

Now that you've talked with some people who are on track with their dreams, you can use what you learned to help someone else, or even a group of people, get a dream going. Step 2 toward the Dream Maker Award asks that you identify a woman or girl (or a group of women and/or girls) who would benefit from your assistance in realizing a dream.

Let's face it: Dreams get stuck all the time, kind of like a call or message you forgot to return. As weeks or even months go by, it gets even harder to follow up. You're too busy or too tired, or just don't have enough resources or support. You can likely find lots of women and girls in your community who have dreams they're having trouble realizing—for all the same reasons: lack of time, energy, resources, or support. So who might you choose to help to earn your Dream Maker Award?

Answering the following questions is sure to lead you to some adoption-worthy dreams!

Who do you see each day as you go to school? Bus drivers? School workers? Busy moms? Delivery people? Who do you see at your community center, gym, or place of worship? Can you see how, with a little exploring, you might find out what they hope for? And then, do you see how, with research and planning, you could help move forward one of these women's dreams?

CAN'T FIND A WHO?
SEARCH FOR A WHERE!

If finding a dreamer to "adopt" sounds like searching for a needle in a haystack, take a step back. Consider what particular "dream areas" might interest you most. For example, if you're an aspiring artist, you may want to assist someone who dreams of being an artist, too. You might find your dreamer by contacting arts organizations or arts councils, or attending an art walk. Want to help some women break into fashion? Contact a fashion school in your area to locate a student struggling to get her work in the public eye. Maybe you want to work with a girl who dreams of playing soccer on her school's all-male team? You can find her, too—by going to the logical place she would hang out: a community soccer field.

By choosing a dream that really speaks to you, you'll not only be helping a dreamer, you'll be gaining experience about how dreams are achieved in a field that you have aspirations in—how dreamy is that?

HOW DO YOU KNOW WHEN YOU'VE SELECTED THE RIGHT DREAM TO ADOPT?

* Does it feel right in your gut?

* Is the person open to assistance?

* Do you feel you can bring something to the table?

* Will it give you an opportunity to plan and support, and therefore hone your leadership skills?

* Do you truly care about this person? About her dream?

* Is this a serious endeavor?

* Do you respect this person, and does she respect you?

* Do you believe in her?

ONCE YOU FIND A POTENTIAL DREAMER . . .

When you find a potential dreamer you might like to "adopt," take some time to talk with her about this *bliss* journey you are on and what is involved in your earning the Dream Maker Award. Then let her know, briefly, why you are interested in her and ask to schedule more time to talk with her.

Think of this next meeting as an informal interview. Start by telling your potential dreamer why she interests you and ask to hear more about her passions and her aspirations. Have some questions ready that will inform you about her potential dreams and let you get to know her. After all, the more you know about someone, the better prepared you will be to help move her dreams forward. You might ask:

✻
What is your daily life like, and where in that life do your passions and aspirations show themselves?

✻
When you think about your passions and aspirations, do you connect any dreams to them?

✻
What would success at this dream mean for you? What would it look like?

✻
Have you set a timeline for that success— a date by which you want to accomplish you dream?

✻
Have you ever tried to plan out, step by step, how you might reach that dream?

✻
What steps, if any, have you already accomplished toward this dream? What steps might you be stalled on?

✻
Where do you think you need the most assistance in pushing this dream forward? Have you thought about what sort of assistance you need?

YOU MAY NEED TO DIG A LITTLE

Some women and girls may not be able to articulate every aspect of their dream right off the bat. If your dreamer isn't yet even sure of her dream, you may first need to help her get focused on what her dream really is. So try to stay focused on getting an answer to this question: *What is the end goal that you want for yourself?*

DECIDING IF THIS IS THE RIGHT DREAMER FOR YOU

If your time with the dreamer makes you want to help her, let her know how much it would mean to you if you could be part of making her dream a reality. Ask if she's willing to be your adopted dreamer.

If she is, thank her and let her know you'd like to now help her take the next step toward her dream. This is where you want to get a dialogue started so that the next step is one your dreamer is comfortable with and willing to take, and one that will move her dream forward. Based on your conversation with your dreamer, you may have some ideas to share with her right now. Or you and your dreamer may want to go off and brainstorm separately. It could be that you want to seek out other successful women in the same (or an even remotely similar) field to learn about specific next steps in this dream.

IDENTIFY YOUR ROADBLOCKS!

As you get to know your dreamer, you may find that her dream was put on hold because of a roadblock or two, such as issues with:

* focus
* not having a step-by-step plan
* support/role models
* resources, including space and time

* knowledge/expertise
* network
* confidence
* societal expectations (gender, cultural)

You may notice some others, too.
Do you recognize any of these roadblocks in your own life?
If so, start moving past them!

If she isn't, or if this dream doesn't seem like the right dream to "adopt," thank the dreamer for her time. Don't feel uncomfortable being direct and honest. Let her know that the time spent with her will still be useful as you go forward with your Dream Maker Award.

Then, move on and explore another (or more) possible dreamer(s), using all the same tips given above! When you've selected a dreamer, use this chart to record your thoughts.

DREAMER . . . .

DREAM   WHY I CHOSE THIS DREAM

HELPING A TEAM
OF WOMEN
MOVE A DREAM FORWARD

A group of ambitious Ambassadors with a passion for cooking decides it wants to help women whose dream involves making and selling great food. So they check with cooking instructors of continuing education classes at a local community college. One of the instructors suggests that the Ambassadors get in touch with a woman named Miki, who has been taking Asian cooking classes for several years, and has mentioned that she has always wanted to cook professionally. Once they find Miki, who is 38, she leads them to her two friends, Kim-Ly, 46, and Adina, 41. All three are enthusiastic home cooks who love to experiment with bold, fresh takes on the traditional Asian dishes that are a part of their heritages.

STEPS OF THE DREAM PLAN

With the Ambassadors' assistance, Miki, Kim-Ly, and Adina write a mission statement that clearly sets out their dream. They choose this wording: *Our dream is to share our passions for healthful Asian fusion food and fresh, locally grown, organic ingredients with our community in a way that also allows us to help support our families.* With the Ambassadors as a sounding board, Miki, Kim-Ly, and Adina weigh the pros and cons of various business ventures: restaurant, catering company, stall at a farmers' market, or food truck.

LIKE TO THINK BIG?

This Sample Dream Maker Project may just whet your appetite!

One of the girls mentions that she saw a crowd gathered around a taco truck at a street fair in her neighborhood. It turned out to be selling tacos inspired by Korean barbecue. The girls and Miki, Kim-Ly, and Adina search "taco trucks" on the Internet and learn more about the boom in the mobile food movement, in which trucks offer great food conveniently and at reasonable prices. They love the idea.

The women create a menu of noodle dishes and devise recipes.

TEST AT A FARMERS' MARKET

The Ambassadors help arrange for Miki, Kim-Ly, and Adina to share a booth with a food vendor at a farmers' market to test their dishes. The feedback is good, but everyone agrees that the noodle dishes aren't the neatest to serve or eat. Plus, they realize they need a heartier vegetarian option. They re-test the next week at the farmers' market with rousing success!

ARRANGING THE FOOD TRUCK RENTAL

Miki, Kim-Ly, and Adina are ready to roll!

WHAT ELSE THE DREAMERS ARE INSPIRED TO DO

Developing the Brand: Miki, Kim-Ly, and Adina move forward with brand development, putting their name and logo on aprons, caps, and, most important, the food truck! Meanwhile, the Ambassadors use their tech skills to design a Web site for the women and inspire them to use social media sites to communicate their hours and locations, so they set up on Facebook and Twitter, too.

DEFINE
THE DREAM

Putting your "adopted dream" down on paper in a way that makes it tangible is your next step toward the Dream Maker Award. First, you will write a mission statement for the dream and then you'll create a step-by-step plan for it. These two parts are equally important.

Writing down a dream's purpose and goal help keep the dream focused. And once you have a dream's purpose and goal written out, you can begin to map all the steps needed to achieve the dream. So, Step 3 toward your Dream Maker Award is the time to take your head out of the clouds and get practical: Do some research, think critically, and problem solve. **Dream big, and then buckle down to accomplish your goals: That's what all great leaders do!**

FIRST, THE MISSION STATEMENT

You'll want to talk with your dreamer(s) so that together you can draft a mission statement that clearly sets out the desired dream.

Just as writing your own mission statement gave you a chance to say who you are, what's important to you, and where you want to go—all in one neat story line—a mission statement for your adopted dream gives you and your dreamer the opportunity to state the dream, why its important, and what its success will be.

Look back at page 59 of the *Live It!* side of this journey. That's where you drafted a mission statement for yourself. Then look at the mission statements in the sample Dream Maker Projects on pages 14, 22, and 28 of this *Give It!* side of the journey. You can see that mission statements take a bird's-eye view of a dream: They look at them from a high level of what the dreamer(s) aspires to. They don't get too nitty-gritty.

See what you might borrow from your experience in writing a mission statement and from the project examples to help inform the mission statement of your adopted dream. Then get going and write it out!

Dream Maker

1. Mission Statement for My "Adopted Dream"

SECOND, DRAFT THE STEPS TO THE DREAM

Keep in mind that stepping out a dream means really taking time to think about, research, and plan how you can get some momentum going for the dream. You'll want to make each step in the dream plan as specific as possible, so that you and your dreamer can easily stay on track and understand what needs to be accomplished.

Think of each step as a rung on a ladder that reaches for the clouds and your dreamer's ultimate bliss.

So how do you get started stepping out the plan? One way is to answer some questions that are bound to lead to steps in your plan:

✳ *Who does the dreamer need to meet, talk to, or network with?*

✳ *What information does she need? Where can that information be found?*

✳ *What might need to change about the dreamer's daily life so that she can carve out time for her dream? What can be done to make these changes happen?*

✳ *What resources does the dreamer need? Who might help provide them?*

A PLAN FOR YOUR DREAMER IS A PLAN FOR YOU!

By the way, this simple and practical way to plan can be useful to you in just about everything you decide to do in life! College search and applications? Job search? Summer trip? Girl Scout Gold Award? And, oh yeah—your own dream plan, too!

Can you see how your answers lead you to some solid steps in your dream plan? Use the chart below to step out the dream. Dates don't have to be exact for all steps, but it's important to settle on a firm date(s) for the step(s) you will help the dreamer accomplish. After you list the steps toward the dream, consider these questions:

* *Does the plan work for the dreamer?*

* *Where might the plan feel too hard?*

* *Where might it need more detail?*

* *Is there a clear and meaningful first step? Is it enough to get momentum going?*

Keep in mind that dream plans are likely to vary widely. So be sure to let the dream be your guide, and to scale and scope your plan to what is practical and doable. If it's not, it's not a good plan! Go back and break down the dream into more doable steps.

2. Steps to Achieving My "Adopted Dream"

Dream Maker

TEP	WHY NEEDED	DATE TO BE ACCOMPLISHED	COMPLETION
			☐
			☐
			☐
			☐

BRINGING
2 PASSIONS TOGETHER

A group of Ambassadors decides to help a younger girl because they remember that when they were younger they had dreams that weren't taken seriously. They appreciate how people are taking their dreams more seriously now and think younger girls should have that experience, too. They all love fashion, so they choose Liliana, 14, a younger cousin of one Ambassador in the group, who dreams of becoming a fashion designer.

When Liliana was 11, she started a fashion blog that she's kept up ever since. She carries her camera wherever she goes to capture pictures of girls and women in cool outfits. Her smart phone is loaded with a gazillion fashion apps. The Ambassadors meet with Liliana to talk about her passion for fashion. Liliana shows them her blog, which combines a diary of her eclectic clothing and accessory choices, her street fashion photos, and her design sketches.

THE GROUP REALIZES THAT LILIANA HAS TWO PASSIONS SHE CAN COMBINE INTO ONE:

As the group spends time with Liliana, the Ambassadors are all distracted from her awesome fashion sense by the amazing amount of technology (and all the cords!) that she's also wearing. "You tell us you have this passion for fashion," they say, "but you have all this stuff hanging off you! Don't you think you should clean up your look?" Liliana, taken aback, defends her love of technology. This triggers the group to start thinking about how technology and not just fashion may be in Liliana's future. "Why don't you combine your two interests?" one Ambassador finally asks. "I know I could use some stylish clothes that would also carry all my tech toys! I'd definitely be one of your customers!"

WRITE A MISSION STATEMENT

With the group's guidance, Liliana sees that her dream is to do more with fashion than simply answer the question "What should I wear today?" Together they write this mission statement: *My dream is to combine my interests in fashion and technology in a way that takes the fashion world to new heights.*

SUGGEST AN INTERNSHIP

The Ambassadors encourage Liliana to build on and develop her technological know-how to match her fashion savvy. One Ambassador tells her about her past experience as an intern at a high-tech firm. This gets Liliana excited. Together, all of them check out the firm's Web site and see that it's offering the internship program again this year.

ASSIST WITH THE INTERNSHIP APPLICATION

The Ambassadors encourage Liliana to apply and help her with the application, which is due in one week.

WHAT ELSE THE DREAMER IS INSPIRED TO DO

The Ambassadors inspire Liliana to submit her designs to her town's Fashion Week, which offers her the opportunity to showcase her work to area buyers and the media.

GIVE IT! GIFT IT!

No matter what dreamer and dream you are assisting, you have one final step to take toward the Dream Maker Award: **Step 4 asks you to move this dream forward and gift its plan to your dreamer.**

THE GIFT OF A DREAM

Gifting the dream plan to your dreamer is a symbol of continued encouragement. So you'll probably want to turn that plan into something you would be proud to present. Be sure to give yourself enough time to be creative so the plan is ready to give at the journey's final celebration!

What forms of creative expression have you explored on this journey that might inspire a way to present your dreamer's steps? How might you make it a plan to cherish?

HERE ARE SOME IDEAS

Cut out the words to the steps from a variety of sources related to your adopted dreamer's dream and then piece them together in a creative way. For example, if your dreamer is an aspiring chef, find all the words in the take-out menus of restaurants in your area and then glue them to a place mat or serving tray. Lacquer the whole thing so it's a waterproof dream plan that your dreamer can use every day!

If your dreamer is an aspiring painter, type or write out the steps toward the dream and cut them into small pieces that you can roll or fold and then place in the compartments of a paintbox.

Now dream up some ideas of your own!

A GIFT THAT KEEPS ON GIVING

For every one dream you can name, there may be hundreds—even thousands!—of women in the world who share that dream. If you have the energy and the desire, let the needs of your dreamer be the catalyst for a wider community of dreamers! The work you do toward keeping these dreams going may just lead you to ideas for your Gold Award project.

So take a look at the examples below. Then, with your sister Ambassadors, see if you can lift some of the steps on your dreamer's path into something that might move even more people toward their dreams!

1 Consider Miki, Kim-Ly, and Adina, who started their food truck. If you were helping with this dream, you might organize a PR workshop for all aspiring business owners (and current owners, too), taught by local experts, that focuses on creating smart logos that will stay in the public's mind. Once the workshop takes place, the women who attend can keep similar business-savvy workshops going on their own with other local experts.

VOW TO STAY IN TOUCH!

Whether through a periodic coffee date or annual holiday cards, aim to stay in touch with your dreamer! Follow her success and let her know all that you're doing toward achieving your own dreams. After all, her story is now part of your story!

Consider Mira, the photographer, who wants to reach the public. If she were your dreamer, you might set up a Web page that could develop into a full-blown online art community. It could support and promote artists, offer ways for them to chat with one another and share advice, and also be a one-stop shop for the public to learn about local artists and see their work.

Consider Liliana, who just found an interesting internship to apply for. If she were your dreamer, you might start an online listing of local internships and job opportunities in a variety of fields that all area teens could use. This listing could also morph into a real network of peer advisers who reach out and share their internship experiences with other girls at area high schools.

IN THIS WAY, THE ONE DREAM YOU ADOPT REACHES OUT TO BENEFIT A WIDER COMMUNITY. WHO KNOWS? IT MAY EVEN SPARK A FEW NEW DREAMS!

How I might lift up some steps of my adopted dreamer's plan to assist even more dreamers:

THEIR DREAMS,
YOUR STORY

By this time, you've likely landed well beyond the wildest visions of your wildest dreams. You're living them and giving them! Are you feeling blissful yet? Are you feeling proud? You should be!

HOPES.
DESIRES.
DREAMS.
BLISS.

Take a moment to enjoy that bliss and to savor that pride. Now's the time to think about all you've explored and accomplished along this *bliss* journey. If you're an official Dream Maker, you're a leader who has inspired others to reach for their dreams and take steps toward achieving them. In the process, you've shown them how to dream, and how to keep on dreaming.

Consider all the ways your thinking about dreams has changed and expanded. Now you know how to make a dream float higher and support multiple dreamers. How might you expand your vision and your reach as a leader whose bliss is tied, in part, to helping others achieve bliss, too?

Assisting others with their dreams strengthened your own sense of self. **Discovering** that made you feel great, right?

Who else do you want to **Connect** with, to move their dreams forward and to strengthen your own dreams? Will you become an even more courageous dreamer—one who **Takes Action** to further dreams that change the world?

Your story of dreams and bliss has just begun. With every new chapter, you have the chance to encourage the dreams of others. Those dreams will be part of your own story—the story of a blissful and inspiring leader.

GET YOUR STORY STARTED

Now, think up two to three things you can do today to begin working toward your dreams. Do this again next week and the week after, and the week after that, and so on. Keep those dream plans going right here! Just remember, your bliss—and your life story!—can be as far-reaching as your wildest dreams!

Think of your mission statement as your story, one you'll want to carry with you as your dream unfolds step by step and you move forward as a leader in your own life. Knowing who you are, what you want to do, and what your dreams are will certainly put you on the road to bliss. Want to learn even more about yourself and feel even more blissful? Connect with others, and Take Action to move them forward on the road to bliss, too! That's what the *give it!* part of this journey is all about. So go ahead, flip for true bliss!

FLIP!